Machine Driver

Editor: Alexandra Koken
Designer and Illustrator: Andrew Crowson

Copyright © QED Publishing, 2011

First published in the UK in 2011 by
QED Publishing
A Quarto Group company
230 City Road
London EC1V 2TT

www.qed-publishing.co.uk

ISBN 978 1 84835 619 1

Printed in China

A catalogue record for this book is available
from the British Library.

Words in bold are
explained in the
Glossary on page 24.

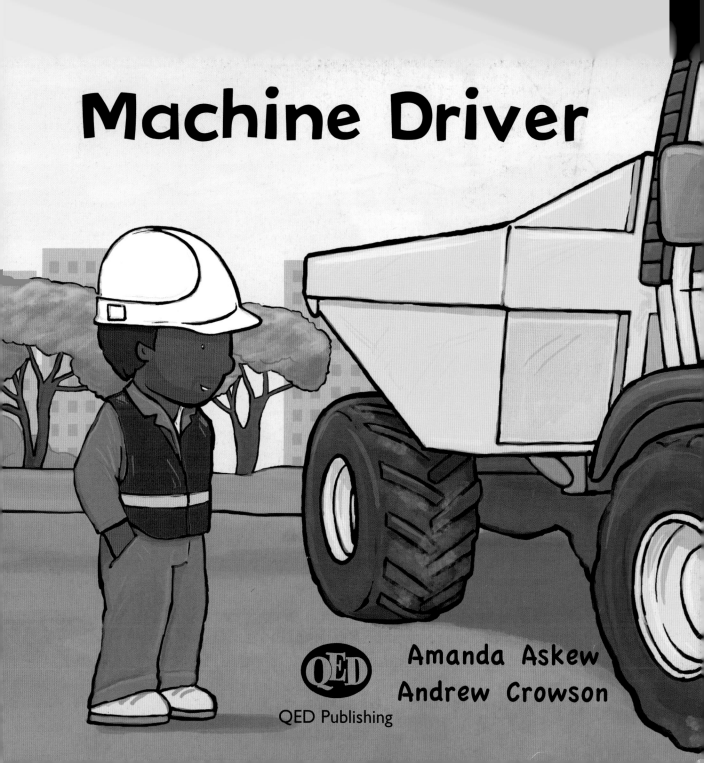

Machine Driver

Amanda Askew
Andrew Crowson

QED Publishing

Meet Andy. He is a machine driver.
The machines he drives help to build
new roads.

Andy arrives at the building site at
6 o'clock in the morning.

Andy wears **overalls**, heavy boots and a hard hat for work. They keep his clothes clean and **protect** his head and feet.

Andy work with a team of machine drivers. He drives a **dump truck**.

Matthew drives a **digger**.

Ryan drives
a loader.

Lauren drives
a roller.

Sam drives a
road-laying
machine.

Sean is in charge. He tells people what to do each day. The team is building a new, wider road next to a school.

"Andy, Matthew and Ryan, please finish clearing the road for the tarmac to be laid. Lauren and Sam, you can lay out the gravel once the road is clear."

"OK, Boss."

Andy climbs up the steps and gets into his cab. He starts the dump truck.

Matthew, Ryan and Andy work together to make the road wider.

Matthew digs up the earth and rubble with his digger. He loads it into the dump truck so that Andy can take it away.

Ryan scoops up the gravel
for the new road. He loads
it into Andy's dump truck.

Andy brings the gravel to be spread out. He drives very slowly and carefully to put it in the right spot.

Lauren and Sam spread out the
gravel with their spades.

"I'm getting hungry!" says Sam.

The team stops working to have a drink and a snack.

It's 8 o'clock. Children are arriving at the school.

Now the team can cover the surface of the road with tarmac. Andy's dump truck pours the tarmac.

Sam's machine spreads out the tarmac.
Lauren's machine rolls out and flattens
the tarmac.

SPLAT! POP! A ball lands on the tarmac
and is squashed by the roller.

"Oh no, my ball!" shouts a boy from
the playground.

Andy, Sam and Lauren turn off
their machines.

Andy picks up the squashed ball and hands it back to the boy.

"There are lots of big machines here. You should be more careful – we don't want anyone to get hurt."

"We will, we promise!"
call the children.

Glossary

Digger A machine with a bucket that is used to dig up earth.

Dump truck A machine with a large container on the back. The container can tip up to pour out its load.

Loader A machine with a bucket on the front. It is used to move heavy materials.

Overalls A one-piece suit worn over clothes to keep them clean.

Protect To stop something from getting damaged.

Road-laying machine A machine that pours tarmac and spreads it out evenly.

Roller A machine with a heavy metal part on the front. It is used to flatten earth and tarmac.

Tarmac A mixture used for building roads. It is made of stones and hot, sticky tar.